CALLIGRAPHY PROJECTS

Fiona Watt and Anna Rowley

Designed by Rebecca Halverson
Illustrated by Jonathan Woodcock

Photographs by Amanda Heywood • Calligraphy by Patricia Lovett
Edited by Felicity Brooks

Contents

Starting out

The word calligraphy is used to describe any kind of beautiful lettering. It comes from two Greek words, *kalli* meaning "beauty" and *graphia* which means "to write". In this book you will find projects which use a variety of different calligraphy techniques.

Equipment

Before you start any of the projects, check that you have all the things you will need. You will probably have some of the equipment, but you may need to go to a craft shop or a stationer's to buy one or two items.

Pens and brushes

You will need a calligraphy pen for some of the projects. There are many different types which you can buy, but the easiest to use are calligraphy felt-tip pens. They are suitable for most of the projects in this book. They have broad, square ends and come in a variety of widths and shades.

You can also buy special metal-nibbed, calligraphy 'dip' pens or fountain pens which you fill with ink or paint. They come with nibs of different widths and produce sharper lines than felt-tip pens. To find out how to use one, follow the maker's instructions, or look in the books listed on page 32. Broad-edge brushes, also known as one-stroke brushes, can be bought at an art supplier's.

Letter styles

On page 32, you will find examples of calligraphy alphabets. The small numbers near to each letter indicate the order in which you make the pen strokes. The arrows show the direction of each stroke. Lift your pen off the paper between each stroke.

There is more information about spacing your letters and how to set out words on pages 30 -31. On these pages there are also details of some of the techniques used in the projects.

Start with line 1. Make the stroke in the direction of the arrow.

1

2

The second stroke also starts at the top.

Finally, add line 3 to complete the letter.

3

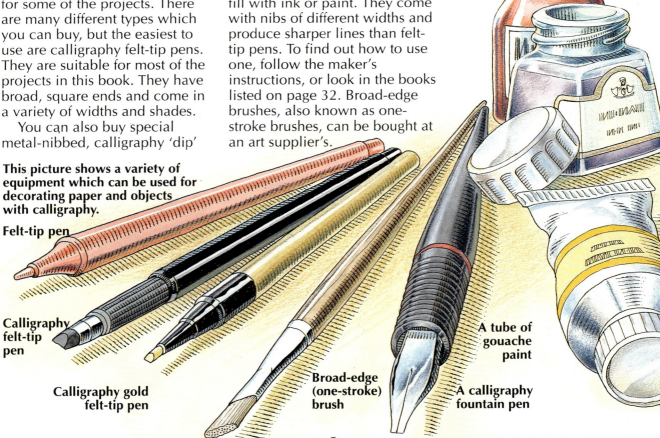

This picture shows a variety of equipment which can be used for decorating paper and objects with calligraphy.

Felt-tip pen

Calligraphy felt-tip pen

Calligraphy gold felt-tip pen

Broad-edge (one-stroke) brush

A calligraphy fountain pen

A tube of gouache paint

Drawing inks

Nib angles

Writing with a broad-edged nib gives you a variety of thick and thin lines. The shape of the letter depends on the angle at which you hold the nib. For most alphabets, the nib should be held at the same angle throughout. The angle is shown by a diagram at the beginning of each alphabet (see page 32).

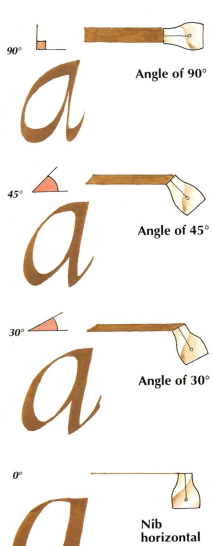

90°

Angle of 90°

45°

Angle of 45°

30°

Angle of 30°

0°

Nib horizontal

Double pencils

To get used to making smooth letter strokes with a calligraphy pen or brush, try taping two pencils together with masking tape. If you are right-handed, place the paper you are working on straight in front of you. If you are left-handed, you may find it easier to place the paper at an angle of about 45° on your work surface (see box below).

Tape two flat-sided pencils together with some masking tape.

If you are left-handed, tape one pencil about 5mm ($^2/_{10}$ in) lower than the other one.

If you haven't tried any calligraphy before, try making simple letter strokes with your double pencils.

Combine the strokes to draw more elaborate patterns.

Fill in the spaces between the lines to see how it would look if you had used a pen.

Left-handers

If you are left-handed, use a pen with a left-oblique nib or double pencils taped as shown above. You may need to change the angle of your wrist or the way you hold the pencils or pen, so that your wrist is under your lettering. Also, try placing your paper at an angle of 45° on your work surface.

Embossed notepaper

Embossing is the shaping or carving of letters or patterns so that they are raised above the surrounding surface.

You will need:

Writing paper and an envelope with a V-shaped flap
2 pieces of thin cardboard the same size as the writing paper
A craft knife
A teaspoon
Double pencils (see page 3)
Paper clips and glue
A fine felt-tip pen

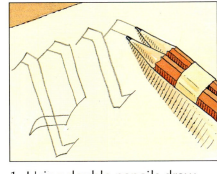

1. Using double pencils draw your initials on one piece of cardboard. Draw them in the same position as you want them to be on your writing paper.

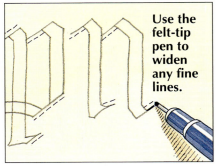

Use the felt-tip pen to widen any fine lines.

2. Make any thin parts of letters about 2mm ($1/16$in) wide, then put some old magazines under the cardboard to protect your work surface.

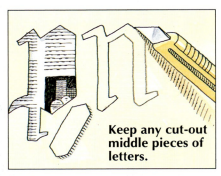

Keep any cut-out middle pieces of letters.

3. Cut out each letter with the craft knife. Then turn the cardboard over and glue it onto the other piece of cardboard. Glue any middle pieces in place.

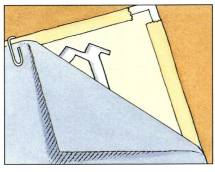

4. Place a sheet of writing paper over the cardboard. Secure it in place with some paper clips. Lay the paper and cardboard on a flat surface.

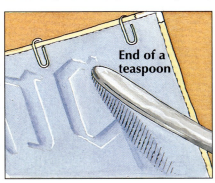

End of a teaspoon

5. Gently push the paper into the cut-out letters, using the end of the spoon. Push right into the edges of the letters to make crisp lines.

6. Carefully remove the paper clips and turn the paper over. You can make many sheets of embossed paper using the same cardboard cut-out.

You could emboss your initials on the cover of a small book. (See pages 24-25 for instructions on how to make a book.)

Embossing an envelope

Use paper clips to attach an envelope to your cardboard cut-out. Make sure that your initials will be the right way up when the envelope is sealed. Use the teaspoon to smooth the flap into the cut-out letters as you did for the writing paper.

Patterns

As well as letters, you can also emboss patterns. Use simple shapes as they are easiest to cut out.

Cards and envelopes

You will need:

Thick, bright paper
Calligraphy pens
Tracing paper
Scissors and a craft knife
Glue
A ruler
Parcel ribbon

Tree card

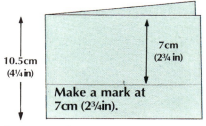

10.5cm (4¼ in)

7cm (2¾ in)

Make a mark at 7cm (2¾in).

1. Cut a piece of paper that measures 10.5 x 28cm (4¼ x 11in). Fold it in half. Draw a faint line 7cm (2¾in) from the top.

To transfer your lettering to the card see page 30.

2. On tracing paper, draw around the front and draw in the faint line. Write your message along the line and on the pot and trunk.

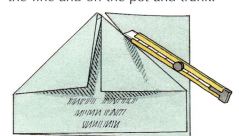

3. Fold the top two corners in so they meet in the middle at the mark on the line. Cut off the top layer of the right-hand flap.

The pattern on the tied card was drawn with a pen and gouache paint (available from an art suppliers).

The hearts on the tree card were drawn with a calligraphy pen.

The lines on the striped, zigzag card were painted in ink using a homemade felt-tip pen (see page 11).

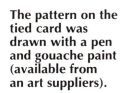

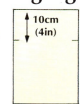

4. You could use a calligraphy pen to draw a pattern on the flaps, or print a design with a rubber stamp (see pages 10 -11).

Zigzag card

10cm (4in)

Turn the paper over.

20cm (8in)

1. Cut a piece of paper 20 x 30cm (8 x 12in). Make pencil marks at 10cm (4in) on one side and 20cm (8in) on the other side.

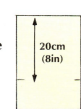

Tied card

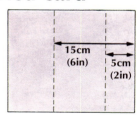

1. Cut a piece of bright paper 24 x 20cm (9½ x 8in). Mark and score lines 5cm (2in) and 15cm (6in) from the right-hand side.

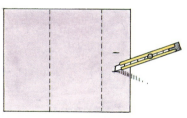

2. Use a craft knife to make two slits, 1cm (½in) long on the narrow section, 8cm (3in) in from each end.

 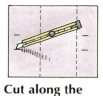

Open out the paper.

Cut along the scored slits.

3. Fold in the flaps, with the narrow one on top. Slide the craft knife through each slit to score lines on the layer below.

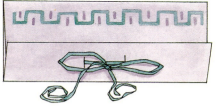

4. Decorate the front and the inside of the card. Thread a piece of parcel ribbon through both sets of slits and tie a bow.

Envelopes

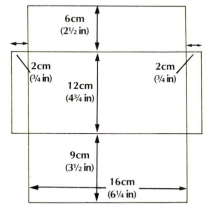

6cm (2½ in)

2cm (¾ in)

12cm (4¾ in)

2cm (¾ in)

9cm (3½ in)

16cm (6¼ in)

The tree card will fit in this size.

1. Copy the measurements above onto paper using a ruler and pencil. If you want to make an envelope for the other cards, change the width of the large rectangle from 16cm (6¼in) to 21cm (8½in).

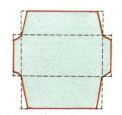

Cut around the outline shown in red.

2. Mark points 1cm (½in) from each corner. Join these points to the corners of the middle rectangle.

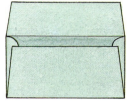

To seal the envelope, stick the top flap with a little glue.

3. Score lightly along each line and fold in the sides. Fold up the bottom. Stick this to the sides with some glue.

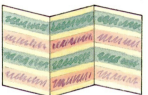

Decorate the front and write your message on the back.

2. Lightly score the paper along the marks you have made. Fold it first one way and then the other to make a zigzag.

A concertina birthday book

You will need:

2 pieces of stiff cardboard
10 x 17cm (4 x 6¾in)
A sheet of paper 56 x 15cm
(22 x 6in) for the pages
2 pieces of giftwrap 14 x 21cm
(5½ x 8½ in)
4 pieces of 25cm (10in) ribbon
A glue stick
A calligraphy pen
A ruler and a craft knife

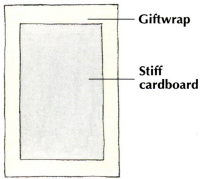
Giftwrap

Stiff
cardboard

1. To make the two covers, cut the cardboard and giftwrap to the correct sizes, using a craft knife and ruler. Glue the cardboard in the middle of the giftwrap, leaving equal margins all around.

Leave a small gap at the corners.

2. Use scissors to trim the corners off the giftwrap, close to, but not touching the corners of the cardboard. Fold the giftwrap over the edges and glue them down carefully.

Front

Back

3. Use glue to stick the ribbons onto the inside of each cover. Make sure there is an equal amount of ribbon at each side. Trim each end diagonally to stop the ribbons from fraying.

Fold the paper into a concertina.

4. Make faint pencil marks every 8cm (3in) at the top and bottom edges of the long strip of paper. Neatly score and fold the paper one way and then the other at each set of marks (see page 31).

You could decorate the covers with lettering or embossing (see pages 4-5), rather than using giftwrap.

(see pages 4-5)

Lettering Styles

You could use a single large letter instead of the whole word for each month. Decorate the inside of the letter with ink or paint in a contrasting shade.

The first page will be January, the sixth will be June. Leave the seventh page blank.

5. Rule double lines along the top for the name of each month. The distance between the lines depends on the size of your nib (see page 30). Write the names of the months between the lines.

(see page 30)

6. Measure out the same lines on the other side. The lettering for July will be on page 8 and so on. December will be on page 13. Leave page 14 blank as this will be stuck to a cover.

7. When you have finished lettering both sides, use glue to stick page 14 in the middle of the front cover. Glue page 7 onto the back cover. Tie the ribbons to close the book.

Giftwrap and tags

You can use calligraphy to decorate large sheets of paper, such as brown parcel paper. You could also experiment with giftwrap that has a simple pattern on it. Before you start, calculate roughly how much paper you will need to wrap your present.

Rubber stamps

You will need:

A large eraser
A craft knife
Tracing paper
A soft and a hard pencil
Double pencils (see page 3) or a calligraphy pen
A large sheet of paper
An ink pad from a stationer's

Gold ink used with a homemade pen (see right)

Brown parcel paper printed with a rubber stamp

Stripes drawn with a felt-tip pen and a cotton-tipped stick, then printed with a rubber stamp

1. Draw around the eraser onto the tracing paper. Draw a letter or shape inside the outline, using the pencils or a pen.

Use some of your giftwrap to make a matching tag.

2. Turn the tracing paper over, place it on the eraser. Use a hard pencil to transfer the lettering to the eraser (see page 30).

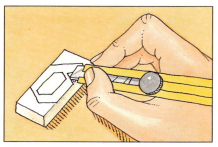

3. Put the eraser on a cutting surface (see page 31). Carefully cut around the outline of the letter or shape using a craft knife.

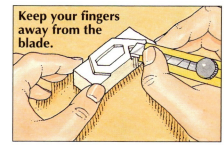

Keep your fingers away from the blade.

4. Carefully slice away the area around the letter, so that the letter stands about 2mm ($\frac{1}{16}$in) above the surface of the eraser.

Homemade pens

You will need:

A craft knife
Thick cardboard
Plastic food wrap
Felt
A rubber band
2 cotton-tipped sticks
Ink or paint

Plastic food wrap —

Felt —

Cut the cardboard into a strip 15 x 2cm (6 x ¾in). Wrap some food wrap around one end of it. Cut a strip of felt the same width as the cardboard. Secure it over the end of the cardboard with a rubber band. Dip the pen into ink or paint and write with it. For smaller letters, cut a narrower strip.

You can also make a double-nibbed pen using the same method. Once you have secured the food wrap and the felt, cut a V-shape into the end of the pen, through the layers.

Use a cotton-tipped stick as a pen, or tape two together to make a thicker pen. Try using this with ink instead of using a felt-tip pen.

Fluid writing

Another technique is to use artists' masking fluid from an art supplier's, with a homemade pen (see right).

Paint the fluid onto paper. When it is dry, sponge ink over it and leave it to dry.

Gently rub the surface of the masking fluid with your finger or an eraser to reveal your lettering.

5. Press the rubber stamp onto the ink pad. Try out various repeated patterns before printing onto your large piece of paper.

An interlocking gift box

You will need:

2 sheets of cardboard, about the
thickness of a cereal box, in
contrasting shades
A craft knife and scissors
Glue
Tracing paper
Calligraphy pen or a broad-
edge brush and paint
A ruler
An eraser

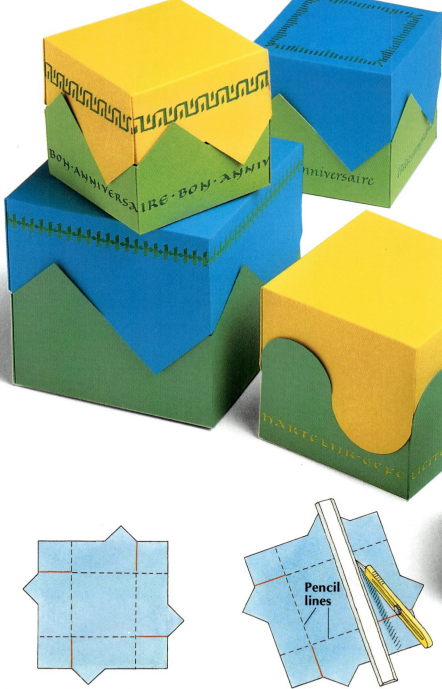

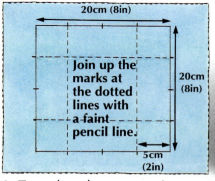

1. To make a box measuring
10 x10cm (4 x 4in), start by
drawing a 20 x 20cm (8 x 8in)
square on both pieces of
cardboard. Measure and mark
points lightly in pencil every
5cm (2in) along each side.

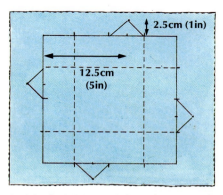

2. Mark 12.5cm (5in) along each
side on both squares. Draw a dot
2.5cm (1in) above each of these
marks. Join each dot to the marks
on the square either side of it.

3. Using a craft knife and a ruler,
carefully cut out the two halves
of the box along the outlines.
Also cut along the red lines
indicated in the picture.

4. Gently score along all the
dotted lines shown above with
a craft knife (see page 31).
Remove all your pencil lines
from each box with an eraser.

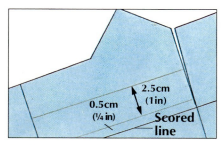

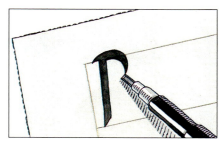

5. Decorate your box before you stick it together. Draw two faint pencil lines 0.5cm (¼in) and 2.5cm (1in) from the scored lines, as guidelines for the letters.

To make a box with wavy edges, open a pair of compasses to 2.5cm (1in) and draw a semicircle at the 12.5cm (5in) mark (see stage 2).

6. Trace over the guidelines onto a piece of tracing paper. Use the guidelines to help with the sizing and spacing of your lettering (see page 30).

7. Transfer the lettering to the side or top of the lid (see page 30). Use either a pen or a broad-edge brush and paint for the lettering.

8. Fold up the edges and bend each tab at right angles to the fold. Glue the tabs inside.

9. Finally, interlock the two halves, making sure that all the triangles are on the outside.

Different-sized boxes

To make a box of a different size, draw a square with sides twice as long as you want them to be when the box is complete. To find out the distance between the marks in step 1, divide the length of the side by four. The height of the points in step 2 is half the distance between these marks.

Mugs and a bowl

You will need :

A plain china mug
Ceramic paint which hardens in
an oven (available in craft shops)
Tracing paper
Clear book-covering film
A craft knife and scissors
An old toothbrush
Double pencils (see page 3)
Paper towels
A ballpoint pen
A small, clean plastic container
Old newspapers
A black felt-tip pen
Masking tape

You could save the letters you
cut out at step 4 and use them
to decorate a matching plate
(see pages 22-23).

Remember to harden
the paint on your
finished object by
following the paint
maker's instructions.

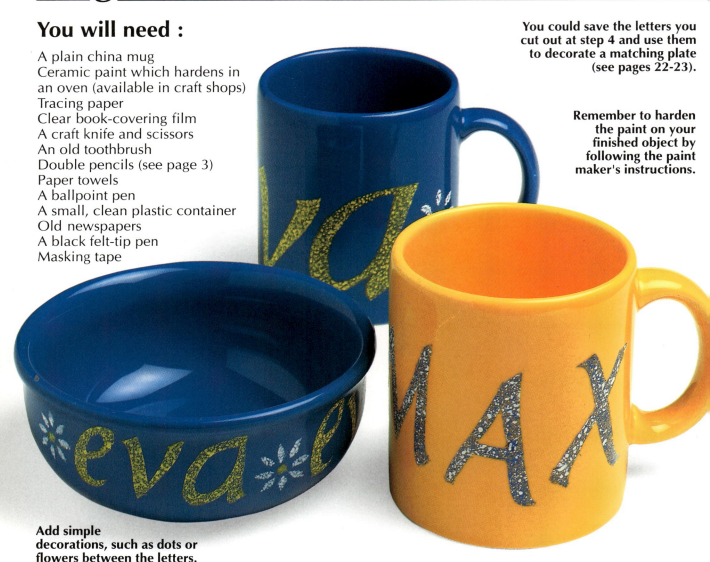

Add simple
decorations, such as dots or
flowers between the letters.

Tracing
paper

1. Cut a strip of tracing paper
about the same height as your
mug and long enough to fit
around it.

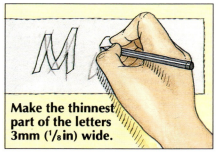

Make the thinnest
part of the letters
3mm (¹/₈in) wide.

2. Using double pencils, write a
message or a name to fit on the
tracing paper. Outline the
letters with a black felt-tip pen.

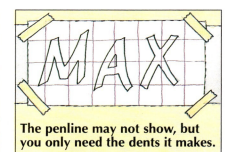

The penline may not show, but
you only need the dents it makes.

3. Cut some film to fit over the
tracing paper. Tape it, shiny side
upward, over the letters. Trace
around them with a ballpoint pen.

4. Place the film on a cutting surface. Use a craft knife to cut out the letters. Keep any middle pieces from the letters as you will need to stick them on the mug.

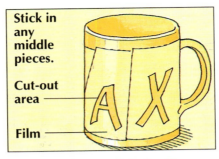

Stick in any middle pieces.

Cut-out area

Film

5. It is easier to stick the film onto the mug if you cut the film into smaller pieces before peeling off the backing paper. Be careful not to cut the letters.

6. Completely cover the rest of the mug, including the handle with pieces of tape. Put lots of paper towels inside the mug so that it is kept clean.

7. In the plastic container, mix a little ceramic paint with water until it is like thin cream. Cover an area with newspaper and put your mug in the middle of it.

8. To spray the letters, dip the toothbrush into the paint and hold it near the mug. Flick your fingernail along the bristles until the letter spaces are covered.

9. You could add another shade of paint once the first has dried. When all the paint is dry, peel off the film. Follow the maker's instructions to harden the paint.

Decorating a bowl

You can use exactly the same technique to decorate the outside of a bowl. To calculate the length of your message, cut a strip of tracing paper long enough to fit around the outside of the bowl.

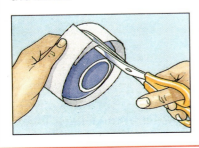

More mugs

Buy a mug with stripes on it. Draw parallel lines, the same width as the stripes. Draw a pattern between the lines then trace it onto the film.

Draw a simple calligraphy pattern (see page 19) and spray it around the base of the mug. Add small dots in a different shade with a fine paintbrush.

Buy a mug with a simple design on it. Trace the shapes onto tracing paper and add letters to fill the spaces. Try putting the letters at at different angles.

Angel decorations and cards

You will need:

Thick white paper 25 x 25cm
(10 x 10in)
A pair of compasses
A pencil and a ruler
Calligraphy pens
A small piece of gold paper
Tracing paper
A needle and thread
A craft knife and scissors

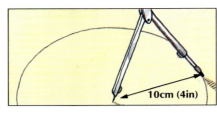

1. Open your compasses to 10cm (4in) and draw a circle on the white paper. The diameter of your circle should be 20cm (8in).

Join the marks to the central point.

2. Divide the circle into quarters with faint lines. Mark points on the outside of the circle 8mm ($^3/_8$in) below the horizontal line.

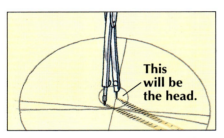

This will be the head.

3. Open the compasses to 1.5cm ($^5/_8$in). Starting with the pencil lead on the central point, draw a circle above the horizontal line.

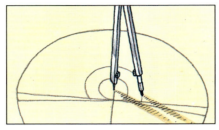

4. Open the compasses to 3cm (1$^1/_8$in) and with the point in the same place, draw an arc between the two sloping lines.

You could make several angels and hang them from different lengths of thread.

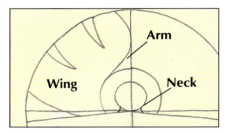

Arm

Wing

Neck

5. Draw the shapes for the wings, neck and arms on one side of the circle as shown on the diagram above.

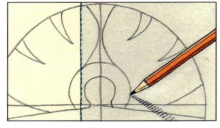

6. Trace around the shapes, turn the paper over and transfer the shapes to the other side of the circle (see page 30).

Transfer the lettering onto the angel.

Buon Natale

7. Trace around the skirt. Write a message which fits in the middle 6cm (2½in) of the skirt, so it can be read when the angel is folded.

8. Cut along all the lines shown in red with a craft knife or scissors. Remove all the pencil lines with an eraser.

Assembling the angel

Fold the wings and the arms forward and roll the arms around a pencil to curl them.

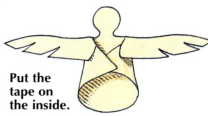

Put the tape on the inside.

Bend the skirt of the angel around to make a cone shape and stick it together with tape.

The angel as a card

To use the angel as a Christmas card, follow steps 1 to 8. Don't forget to include a halo. Either buy an envelope at least 21 x 21cm (8½ x 8½in) to fit the card, or make one following the instructions on page 7, adjusting the measurements so that the middle rectangle becomes a square measuring 21 x 21cm (8½ x 8½in) and the right one measures 21 x 18cm (8½ x 7in).

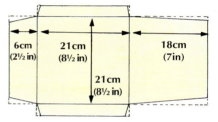

6cm (2½ in)	21cm (8½ in)	18cm (7in)
	21cm (8½ in)	

Copy the instructions from the box (below left) on how to assemble the angel. Send them in the envelope with your card.

Buon Natale

Happy Christmas

Prettige Kerstdagen

Buon Natale

Draw a small circle with a tab on gold paper for the halo. Stick it onto the angel's head.

To make a hanging decoration, push a needle with thread through the top of the angel's head and tie the ends to make a loop.

Decorating a terracotta pot

You will need:

A clean terracotta plant pot
Tracing paper and masking tape
A broad-edge (one-stroke) paint
brush from an art supplier's
Artist's acrylic paints
A plastic lid
Carbon paper (see page 30)
Double pencils (see page 3)
Scrap paper

**Instead of drawing a pattern,
you could write a name
around the pot, or combine
lettering and patterns.**

1. Make sure the surface of the terracotta pot is absolutely clean. If you need to wash it, leave it overnight to dry out as this type of pot absorbs a lot of water.

Leave your pot on a pile of old newspapers to dry out.

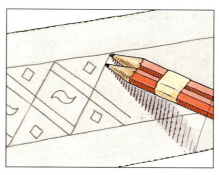
2. To calculate the length of your decoration, cut a strip of tracing paper which fits around your pot. On scrap paper, try out different patterns using double pencils or copy some from below.

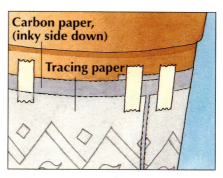
Carbon paper, (inky side down)

Tracing paper

3. Once you are happy with your design, trace it onto the strip of tracing paper. Stick a piece of carbon paper onto the pot, inky side down, then tape the tracing paper over it.

4. Use a pencil with a hard lead to trace over the outline of your pattern (see page 30). Check that it has traced completely before pulling off the papers.

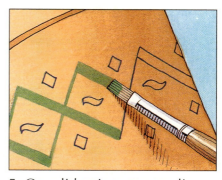
5. On a lid, mix some acrylic paint with water so that it is like thin cream. Paint over the pattern with the brush. Some shades may need two coats of paint.

Depending on the shape of your pot, you could paint your decoration or lettering around the rim or the base of the pot, or both.

Calligraphic patterns

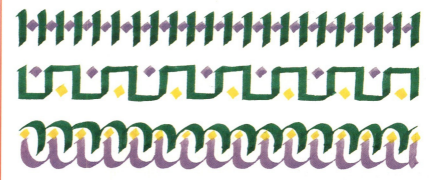

A sun clock

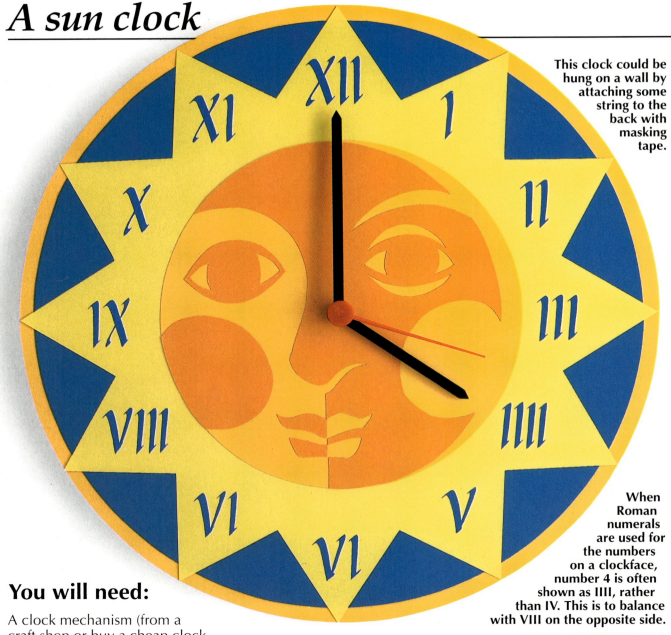

This clock could be hung on a wall by attaching some string to the back with masking tape.

When Roman numerals are used for the numbers on a clockface, number 4 is often shown as IIII, rather than IV. This is to balance with VIII on the opposite side.

You will need:

A clock mechanism (from a craft shop or buy a cheap clock and take it apart)
A piece of thick cardboard
A pair of compasses
Thick, bright paper in blue, orange and two shades of yellow
Calligraphy pens
Tracing paper
A pencil and a ruler
A craft knife and scissors
Masking tape
PVA (household) glue

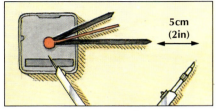

1. Open the compasses so that they are 5cm (2in) wider than the long hand of the clock. Draw a circle on the thick cardboard. Cut it out using a craft knife.

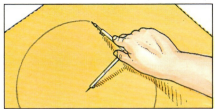

2. Draw a circle the same size as the cardboard on the dark yellow paper and on a piece of tracing paper. Use scissors to cut both of them out.

3. Reduce the width of the compasses by 8mm (³/₈in) and draw a circle on the blue paper. Cut it out, using scissors.

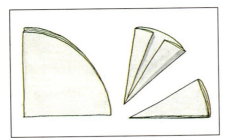

4. Fold the tracing paper into quarters. Then fold it into thirds by bending both edges in so that they overlap. Crease the folds.

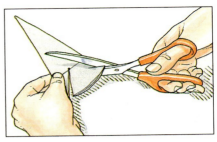

5. Draw a line 4cm (1½in) from the edge of the circle. Make a mark halfway along this line. Cut in from both corners to this mark.

6. Open out the tracing paper and spread it out on the pale yellow paper. Draw around it, then use a ruler to straighten the lines. Cut out the star shape.

7. Set the compasses to 1cm (½in) wider than the short hand. Draw a circle on the dark yellow paper. Cut it out and put it in the middle of the star. Draw around it.

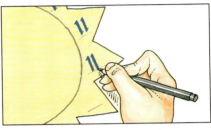

8. Each number fits on one of the points. Either draw them freehand, or try them out on tracing paper and then transfer them to the clock (see page 30).

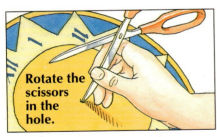

Rotate the scissors in the hole.

9. Glue the circles and the star to the cardboard, starting with the biggest one. Decorate the face (see below). Enlarge the central hole with some scissors.

10. Take the hands off the clock mechanism. Push the spindle of the mechanism through the hole from the back. Replace the hands on the front of the clock.

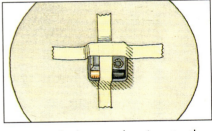

11. Attach the mechanism to the back of the clock with masking tape. If you want to make your clock more durable, paint it with a couple of coats of the glue.

Decorating the face

Make the face after attaching the circles and star in step 9. Begin by cutting an orange circle, the same size as the dark yellow one.

1. Draw in the features marked by the blue line. Cut them out carefully.

2. Glue the main part of the face and the left eye onto the yellow circle.

3. Turn over the pieces for the lips and cheek, and glue them in place.

Calligraphy on a plate

You will need:

A plain china plate
Ceramic paint which hardens in
an oven (from a craft shop)
A pair of compasses
Tracing paper
A ballpoint pen
A black felt-tip pen
Double pencils (see page 3)
Scissors and a craft knife
A sponge
An old plastic lid or paper plate
Old newspapers
Book-covering film

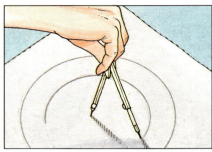

1. Draw around the china plate onto tracing paper. Draw in the rim of the plate by opening the compasses to half the width of the central area of the plate. Cut around the outline of the plate.

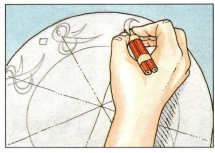

2. Fold the tracing paper into quarters and then in half again. Open it out. Using the creases as a guide for spacing, draw a pattern or lettering around the rim with double pencils.

To fill the inside shape of each bird, trace its outline onto tracing paper and cut it out. Place the tracing paper stencil on the plate and sponge through it.

The letter H was painted with a broad-edge brush.

3. On the tracing paper, draw carefully around your pencil lines with a black felt-tip pen. Make any of the thin parts of your pattern or lettering at least 3mm (1/8in) wide.

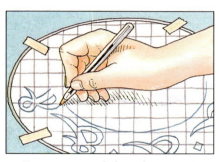

4. Draw around the plate on some book-covering film. Cut it out, then tape it over the tracing paper. Trace over your design using a ballpoint pen. Also draw the inner circle on the film.

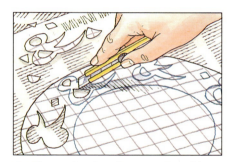

5. Place the book-covering film on a cutting surface (see page 31). Use a craft knife to cut out around the black lines that form your pattern or lettering. Keep all the shapes you have cut out.

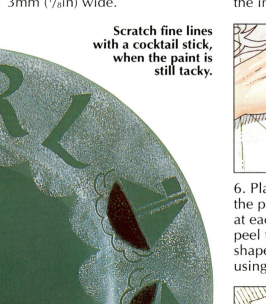

Scratch fine lines with a cocktail stick, when the paint is still tacky.

Use a felt-tip pen to make the marks.

6. Place your tracing paper over the plate and make a tiny mark at each crease. One by one, peel the backing paper off each shape and stick it onto the rim, using the marks as a guide.

7. Use scissors to cut out the central circle from the book-covering film. Peel the backing paper off the circle and stick it very carefully in the middle of the plate.

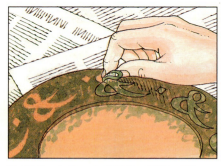

8. Put a little ceramic paint on the plastic lid. Dip the sponge into it and dab it onto some newspaper to get rid of excess paint. Dab the sponge lightly all over the rim of the plate.

9. When the paint is still tacky, carefully peel off the film. It may help to slip the blade of a craft knife under it to start it off. Follow the maker's instructions for hardening the paint.

An address book

You will need:

4 pieces of fairly thick paper 20 x 30cm (8 x12in)
2 sheets of contrasting bright paper 20 x 30cm (8 x 12in)
Thick bright paper 20 x 30cm (8 x 12in) for the cover
A craft knife
A ruler and pencil
75cm (30in) of embroidery thread and a large needle
Calligraphy pens
Glue and masking tape

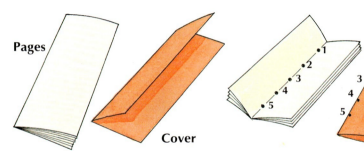

Pages

Cover

1. Fold the four sheets of thick paper in half. Place the pages inside each other to make a book. Score a line down the middle of the cover and fold it.

2. On the inside piece of paper make five light pencil marks at 5cm (2in) intervals along the fold. Do the same on the cover paper and number the marks.

3. Stitching the pages together

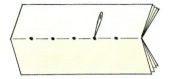

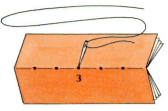

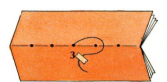

a) Push the needle through the pages at each mark on the fold.

b) Do the same with the cardboard and put it around the pages.

c) Thread the needle and push it through the book at hole 3.

d) Leave about 20cm (8in) loose. Secure it with a little tape.

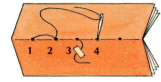

e) Push the needle up through hole 2 and down through 1.

f) Stitch back up through 2 and down through 4.

g) Stitch up through 5, down through 4 and up through 3.

h) Tie the loose ends tightly in a double knot and trim the ends.

Fold back the back cover and pages so that you don't cut through them.

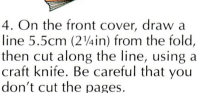

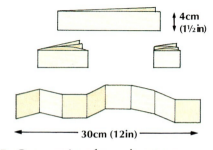

4cm (1½in)

30cm (12in)

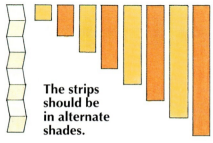

The strips should be in alternate shades.

4. On the front cover, draw a line 5.5cm (2¼in) from the fold, then cut along the line, using a craft knife. Be careful that you don't cut the pages.

5. Cut a strip of rough paper 30 x 4cm (12 x 1½in). Fold it in half three times to give eight equal sections. This will act as a guide for the decorated sections.

6. Cut strips of bright paper 5 x 30 cm (2 x 12in). Using the guide, cut one section from one paper and two sections from the other, and so on.

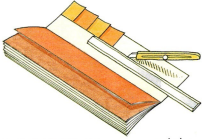

7. Stick the longest strip of bright paper onto the last page in the book. Stick the next longest onto the next page, and so on.

You could print a pattern on the cover with a rubber stamp (see pages 10-11), or cut out the word "ADDRESSES" from a contrasting shade and glue it on.

8. Fold back the cover and the rest of the pages in turn, so you can cut away the excess white paper at the bottom of each strip using a craft knife and a ruler.

Decorating the pages

Draw faint pencil lines at the bottom of each strip for the position of the letters. On rough paper, try out different styles of lettering to fill the spaces.

The 2 longest strips will be STUV and WXYZ, the other strips have 3 letters each.

Use a calligraphy pen to write the letters directly onto the strips, or use tracing paper to transfer your letters (see page 30), then fill them in.

A calligraphy nightshirt

You will need:

A large T-shirt
A large sheet of paper
Fabric paint from a craft shop
Clear book-covering film
A small sponge and a saucer
Masking tape and a craft knife
A large piece of cardboard
Paper towels
A ballpoint pen
A black felt-tip pen
A broad calligraphy pen

How to prepare your T-shirt

The cardboard stops the paint from soaking through to the back.

If the T-shirt is new, wash it to remove any 'finish'. Iron it to remove any creases. Slide the cardboard inside the T-shirt.

Masking tape   Paper towels

Place some paper towels between the front of the T-shirt and the cardboard. Smooth the fabric and secure it to the cardboard using masking tape.

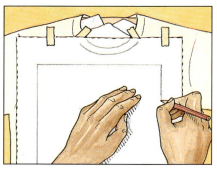

1. Spread the sheet of paper over the T-shirt and draw a rough outline of the area you want to decorate. Draw in the position of the arms and the neck.

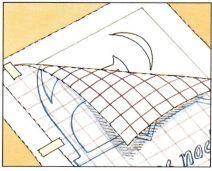

3. Outline your design with a black felt-tip pen. Tape a piece of book-covering film over the whole design, then draw over the lines with a ballpoint pen.

5. Peel the backing paper away from the film at the top. Stick it in place on the T-shirt. Gradually peel the rest of the backing away, sticking it down as you do it.

2. Place the paper onto a flat surface. Design your stencil inside the outline. Use double pencils (see page 3) or a calligraphy pen for the lettering.

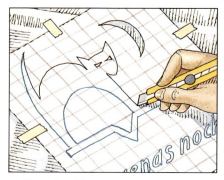

4. Put the film onto a cutting surface. Cut around each letter or shape and remove the pieces to leave a stencil. Keep any middle pieces of letters.

6. Pour some of the fabric paint onto a saucer. Dip the sponge into the paint and then gradually dab it all over the holes in your stencil to fill them in.

This T-shirt is decorated with small, intricate lettering. It is much easier to use large letters and simple shapes, as they are easier to cut out.

You could use the same method to print the name of a sport's team or club onto a T-shirt.

Draw a design to stencil onto boxer shorts or cycling shorts to wear with the nightshirt (see below right).

7. Leave the paint to dry thoroughly before peeling off the stencil. Follow the maker's instructions for 'fixing' the paint, so that the T-shirt can be washed.

Matching shorts

You could also decorate a pair of cycling shorts or boxer shorts in the same way as the T-shirt. Place the shorts onto a piece of paper and draw around them. Draw a design which fits onto the legs of the shorts. Follow the instructions from step 3.

A papier mâché bowl

Papier mâché takes quite a long time to do, but you do not need to do all the stages of sticking on the layers at one time. It also takes several days to dry out, but the results are worth waiting for.

You will need:

A large bowl
Newspaper cut into squares of about 4-5cm (1½-2in)
A small plastic container
Petroleum jelly
Artist's acrylic paints
PVA (household) glue
Emulsion paint
A thick and a fine paint brush
Carbon paper
Tracing paper
Masking tape
Self-adhesive labels
A sponge
A pair of scissors

1. Smear the inside of the bowl with an even layer of petroleum jelly to stop the newspaper from sticking to the bowl.

Overlapping squares around the rim will be cut off later.

3. Lay squares of newspaper all over the greased surface of the bowl. Make sure they overlap each other slightly.

The tinted glue will help you to see each completed layer.

2. In a small container, mix six tablespoons of glue with two tablespoons of water. Tint the glue with a little acrylic paint.

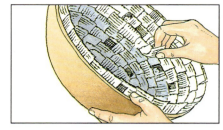

4. Paint the glue mixture gently over the surface and add another layer of squares. Overlap the rim of the bowl by about 3cm (1¼in).

Decorating the inside

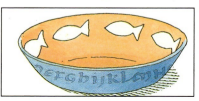

1. Cut out simple shapes from self-adhesive labels. Peel off the backing paper and stick them on at regular intervals.

2. Put some acrylic paint on a saucer. Press the sponge into it and dab the paint over the shapes and the inside.

3. As soon as you have finished sponging on the paint, carefully remove the self-adhesive shapes.

4. Paint the inside of the bowl with two coats of the glue. Allow each coat to dry before painting on the next one.

Add extra layers on the base to stop the bowl from toppling over.

5. Add at least twelve more layers of glue and newspaper to make the bowl strong. Continue to overlap the rim with each layer.

6. Paint a final layer of glue on the inside of the bowl. Leave it in a warm place for two to three days to dry out completely.

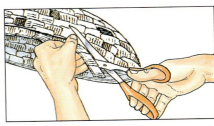

7. Draw a line around the top of the original bowl, then ease out the papier mâché bowl and use scissors to cut around the line.

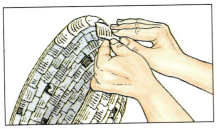

8. Stick squares over the rim to finish off the edge. Add a final layer of squares on the outside to make a smooth surface.

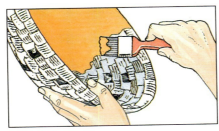

9. When dry, paint the inside of the bowl with emulsion paint, using the large brush. When this has dried, paint the outside.

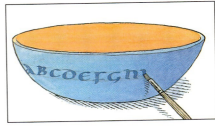

10. Follow the instructions on page 15 to calculate the spacing of the letters on the outside of the bowl. Use acrylic paint for the lettering. Varnish with two coats of glue, allowing it to dry in between.

You cannot wash the bowl, but you can wipe it with a damp cloth to clean it.

Calligraphy and craft techniques

On these two pages you will find most of the techniques which are used in the projects.

Letter height

In each alphabet, the height of a letter is determined by the thickness of your pen nib. At the beginning of the alphabets on page 32, there is a small diagram showing you the number of nib widths the letters should be. This is called the x-height as it is the size of the small letter x in that alphabet. To find the x-height for the nib you are using, hold your pen nib at 90° and make small steps, one above the other.

An x-height of five nib widths.

The part which goes above the x-height is called an ascender.

This part is called a descender.

Measure guidelines using a ruler and a pencil so that the letters, ascenders and descenders are the same height.

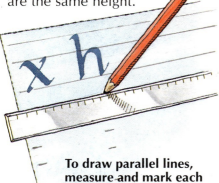

To draw parallel lines, measure and mark each point in at least two places and join the marks.

Spacing

Because letters are different shapes, the spaces between them cannot be measured exactly. Judge the spacing by eye so that it looks even. It's a good idea to try out your lettering on a piece of scrap paper before you work on any object. When you are happy with the spacing, trace over the lettering and transfer it to your object (see below).

Tracing

Once you have found the right spacing for your letters or words, trace around the outline of each letter with a pencil.

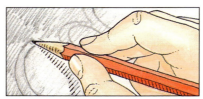

Scribble over the back of the lettering with a soft pencil, such as a B or 2B pencil.

Turn the tracing paper over and secure it in position with masking tape. Trace over the letters with a hard 2H pencil.

If you are using large lettering, draw each letter separately, cut them out and stick them in place.

If your letters are small, leave a gap between each word the width of a letter 'o' in that alphabet.

You can use carbon paper to transfer your lettering. This technique is described fully in the terracotta pot project (see pages 18-19). Dressmakers' carbon paper is best to use because it isn't inky or messy.

If you are going to use a brush to fill in the lettering, draw the outlines of the letters.

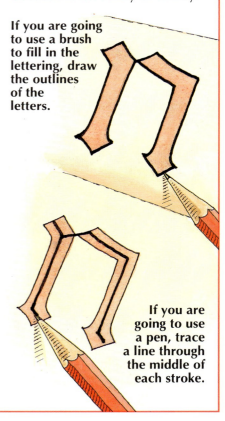

If you are going to use a pen, trace a line through the middle of each stroke.

Layout

The way lettering is arranged on an object is called layout. To place a word centrally, do the lettering on a rough piece of paper. Fold the paper in half to find the middle and trace or copy it onto your object.

Line up lettering to the left or right by cutting words into strips and taping them in position. Then, trace or copy them onto an object.

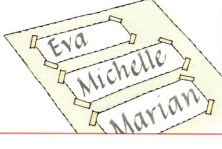

If the word is too long for a space, use a narrower nib and make the lettering smaller.

If a word doesn't fill a space, use a thicker nib and make the letters larger.

Folding paper and cardboard

Lightly fold the paper over, then run the bowl of a clean spoon along the fold to make a crease. To avoid marking your paper, place a piece of thin paper over the fold, then make the crease.

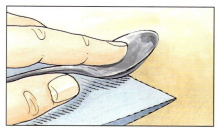

When folding cardboard or thick paper, it is best to score a line to fold along. Put a metal ruler along the line you wish to score, then run a craft knife along it very lightly. Do not cut into the cardboard or paper at all.

When you have scored a line, fold the cardboard or paper along the line. It may help to hold a ruler along the scored line as you make the fold.

Using a craft knife

Always take special care when using a craft knife. Make a cutting surface using very thick cardboard or several old magazines to avoid cutting into the surface below. Try to cut away from the fingers which are holding the paper steady. When cutting a straight line, it is best to use a metal ruler.

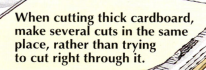

When cutting thick cardboard, make several cuts in the same place, rather than trying to cut right through it.

Calligraphy alphabets

Italic capital letters

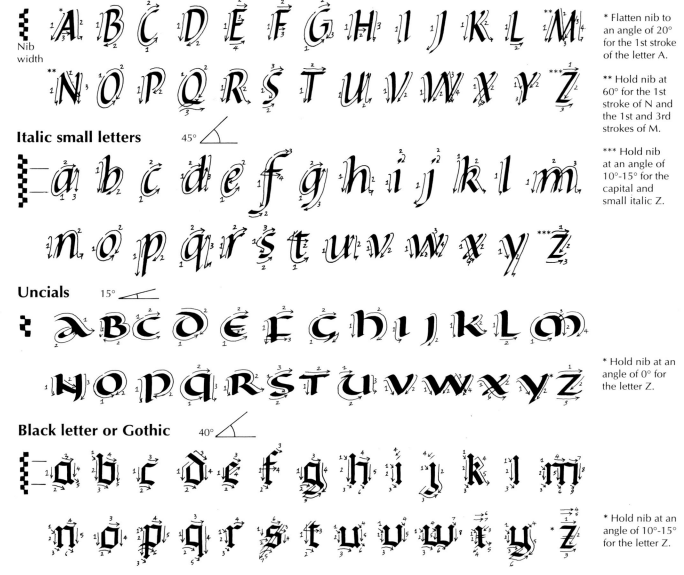

45°

Nib width

* Flatten nib to an angle of 20° for the 1st stroke of the letter A.

** Hold nib at 60° for the 1st stroke of N and the 1st and 3rd strokes of M.

*** Hold nib at an angle of 10°-15° for the capital and small italic Z.

Italic small letters

45°

Uncials

15°

* Hold nib at an angle of 0° for the letter Z.

Black letter or Gothic

40°

* Hold nib at an angle of 10°-15° for the letter Z.

Books to read

Calligraphy - Caroline Young (Usborne).
Teach Yourself Calligraphy - Patricia Lovett (Hodder and Stoughton).
Creating Letterforms - Rosemary Sassoon and Patricia Lovett (Thames and Hudson).
Creative Calligraphy - Rachel Yallop (Hodder and Stoughton).

Groups and societies

Ask in your local library for a list of calligraphy groups. 'Letters' is an international society for young people. It issues a newsletter which contains ideas and projects, and also runs workshops. Send a stamped addressed envelope to Letters, Hernewood, Gracious Lane, Sevenoaks, Kent. TN13 1TJ England for more information.

First published in 1994 by Usborne Publishing Ltd., Usborne House, 83-85 Saffron Hill, London EC1N 8RT, England. Copyright © 1994 Usborne Publishing Ltd. The name Usborne and the device are Trade Marks of Usborne Publishing Ltd. All rights reserved. No part of this publication may be reproduced, stored in a retrieval system or transmitted in any form or by any means, mechanical, photocopying, recording or otherwise, without the prior permission of the publisher. Printed in Portugal. First published in America in March 1995. UE.

745.6